Tacenda

Radnyi Jagtap

BookLeaf Publishing

India | USA | UK

Presentation by *BookLeaf Publishing*

Web: www.bookleafpub.com

E-mail: info@bookleafpub.com

ISBN: 9789363318540

First edition 2024

~ To the wellspring of whispered truths and echoing dreams, to the battleground where vulnerabilities clash and resilience is forged.~

This book is dedicated to my painfully beautiful mind. It is a tribute to the lonely conversations held in the quiet corners of my being, conversations that dared to peel back layers and reveal a self I never fully knew. Through these solitary dialogues, I found the courage to confront the depths, to embrace the complexities, and ultimately, to see myself anew.

ACKNOWLEDGEMENT

Writing the poems in "Tacenda" was a journey of unearthing the unspoken, and it wouldn't have been possible without the whispers of gratitude echoing in my heart.

First and foremost, my deepest thanks go to my muse, the ever-present silence that holds within it a universe of emotions. It's through this silence that the words in these poems find their voice.

To my aunt, Shilpa Shinde, thank you for the unexpected gift of self-reflection. The mirror you held up challenged me to confront depths I may have otherwise avoided. It was a pivotal moment on this journey.

To the situations, both joyful and difficult, you have all been my teachers. You coaxed emotions to the surface, some sweet, some bitter, all of them vital for the creation of these poems.

To my ever-supportive parents, Bhalchandra Jagtap and Prachi Jagtap, your unwavering belief in me has been a constant source of strength. Thank you for always being my safe harbor.

To my English mentors, Dhruv Sir and Ameya Sir, your guidance and dedication nurtured my skills throughout the years. I am forever grateful for the seeds you planted that blossomed into this collection.

To Roshan Somayajula, [my best friend from school], your unwavering encouragement sparked the flame of writing within me nine years ago. I wouldn't be here without you believing in me from the very beginning.

And to EVERYONE who ever said anything extremely positive or nauseatingly negative to me, your words and actions have shaped me in ways both subtle and profound. Thank you for contributing to the tapestry of experiences that have woven themselves into these poems.

Finally, a heartfelt thank you to Bookleaf Publications for believing in "Tacenda" and giving it a platform to reach readers.

And perhaps the most profound acknowledgment of all goes to my own mind. This past year of self-reflection has been a revelation, a journey to discover the wellspring of creativity and the hidden depths of my being. I am forever grateful for its whispers, complexities, and boundless potential.

PREFACE

Remember the introspective wanderings of Reverie? Tacenda takes us on a similar journey, but this time, we delve deeper. Unspoken experiences, passions, and emotions flourish in the rich soil of the unsaid as we delve into the hidden gardens of the heart.

To be silent is to do more than simply not make any noise at all. It's a vibrant language with its own secrets to share. These poems are like delicate flowers, nurtured by the hush that surrounds them.

I, Radnyi, act as your guide on this exploration. With words as my trowel, we'll unearth the complexities of unspoken truths, the silent yearning for connection, and the echoes of experiences that struggle to find voice.

Prepare to embark on a journey where whispers sing. Prepare to be surprised by the profound language that blossoms in the spaces between spoken words. Within these poems lies a mirror reflecting the hidden depths of your being, waiting to be discovered.

Tacenda, in contrast to the tranquility of "Reverie," invites interaction. It beckons you to accept your silent selves and make peace with the dormant parts that want to blossom.

So,
Dearest Reader,
I implore you, to please not read my poems in your predicaments !!

~ Radnyi

~ prelude ~

Maybe a few decades later,
You'll still find me in the notes,
Vehement typing on the display,

Emptying my mind,
inside those sinches,
Lost in my own poetries,

Words comforting me through,
The good, bad, and the tragically beautiful...

Homeless

With 67 kilos, a life contained,
I bid farewell to my loved ones, heart in pain.
Friends joined the chaos, packing, laughter spun,
Meaningless words, roasts, jokes on the run.

But laughter dimmed, replaced by salty tears,
Seeing their faces, etched in fading years.
That Arcade echoed with a final jest,
A hug held tight, against my yearning chest.

Onlookers saw drama, teenage woes,
Unseen, the heart's weight, nobody knows.
Each step back home, a heavier tread,
87 hundred miles, a future yet unshed.

Numbness embraced me in the airport's hold,
Mom's hug, a void, yet warmth untold.
As engines roared, wings lifted high,
My heart, shattered against the cashmere, in the sky.

Ten months have passed, like seasons in decay,
Freedom's dream, where home is far away.
But somewhere deep, amidst the search and chase,
A yearning whispers, "Homeless in this space."

Depth of Darkness

Cobblestones gleam, slick with the city's sheen,
Alien stars paint an unfamiliar sky.
Home's hearth a memory, embers unseen,
Lost in labyrinthine whispers, where shadows
lie.

Tongue stumbles, searching for comfort's sound,
Walls whisper tales in an unheard tongue.
Loneliness echoes, a wolf unbound,
Moonlight a predator, coldly clung.

But in the dark, a resilience blooms,
A strength unfurled in uncharted space.
Stars, once foreign, weave whispered rooms,
And depths of darkness become a familiar
embrace.

Humbled Down

Exalted lowliness, a child of grace,
Raised humble-proud, a paradox in place.
Mirrors reflect a gilded sheen,
But self-worth's whisper, faint and unseen.

A deafening silence in the hall of praise,
A brilliant failure in achievement's maze.
Ten on a scale, the world might decree,
Yet in my eyes, a glorious mediocrity.

This learned restraint, this muted song,
A hopeful yearning to forever belong.
Perhaps one day, the scales will tip,
And love's own light will mend this self-inflicted
rip.

…dreams

Neon dreams still beckon down that weary,
moonlit lane,
But melodies of heartache echo back in
mournful strain.
No asphalt paradise waits, just shattered shards
of light,
Where aspirations wither, lost in shadows of the
night.

The jukebox plays on repeat, a chorus of despair,
While shattered souls like mine in vacant
doorways stare.
We're ghosts along the boulevard, where hope
has gone astray,
Whispers of resilience fading with each passing
day.

Still, amidst the wreckage, embers flicker,
embers fight,
For even broken dreams can mend with
morning's golden light.

to my north through the dissonance

Jumbled within You,
My cogitations find their way,
Amidst the labyrinthine chaos,
Yet, crave to linger and sway...

In the convolutions and twists,
I discover my true north,
The cluttered mosaic of life,
Guides me to where I'm brought forth...

Jumbled within You,
I feel emancipated and alive,
There's no need for perfection,
Just to let the pieces thrive...

Jumbled up in You,
For within Your ardent embrace,
I unearth tranquility in the mess...

because, I would have…

These connections, scattered like ice on a tray,
Half-drunk Starbucks, a flavor gone astray.
We sat, we talked, a promise in the air,
But the warmth never reached us, a friendship
left bare.

The "what ifs" whisper, a haunting refrain,
The paths not taken, the sunshine and rain.
Because I would have danced in the storm by
your side,
Held your umbrella, a shield from the tide.

I dreamt of adventures, laughter unfurled,
Secrets whispered, a loyalty uncurled.
But the moments grew stale, the silence grew
deep,
And the things left unsaid, promises we'd keep.

It stings, a dull ache, a yearning unknown,
For the efforts I'd make, the seeds I'd have sown.
Because I would have listened, a shoulder to
lean,
A champion relentless, fierce, loyal scene.

The "because I would have" a burden to bear,
A ghost of potential hanging in the air.
Where the warmth takes hold, and the "would
have" breaks through.

Fractured

Out the door, a facade crumbles,
Shoulders slump, a weary Atlas,
The weight of the world, a hidden rumble.

Tears streak, a McLaren's chase,
Desperation for a tearful oasis,
To cleanse the heart, to find solace.

Library walls, a refuge sought,
But the soul remembers a heavier cost,
Too many tears, a heart unknot.

Study room, a solitary plight,
What brought this darkness, this endless night?

Was it a friend's careless word?
A roommate's unknowing curd?

Or a stranger's frown, a fleeting slight?
Perhaps a childhood, lost in the fright,
Of being alone, in the dark's tight hold,
A tiny voice, unheard, untold.

Or a bully's shadow, long and vast,
The echo of whispers, a love that couldn't last.

Maybe a promise, a broken vow,
A little girl, left waiting, somehow.

The imposter's mask, a heavy guise,
A self-fulfilling prophecy, in tear-filled eyes.

~ faux pas ~

Tumbled down the crests,
With the luggage loaded up...
And when I let it go, I got my,
Hard landing, into the trough....
Now I'm down to put together,
All that scattered, wherever...
I'd lay still to the rhythmic beat,
Of my own heart, whenever....
Took me long enough to smudge off,
The facade with the breaking sobs...
And then there's a knock on the door,
And I guess they are here to stay...
Pressing pause on that little breakdown,
Even with the smile from eye to eye...
I know, I'm just a faux pas....

...good night, my dear...

Slumber now, little one, beneath the velvet
night,
Let phantoms pirouette, banishing all fright.
Barbed pronouncements and tears like falling
rain,
Sleep shall be a balm, soothing every pain.

Relinquish the anxieties of those who have
flown,
Like autumn leaves scattered, they are simply
wayfarers unknown.
Their absence cannot extinguish the radiance
within,
You are valiant, you are courageous, with a spirit
that cannot be hidden.

Fret not, dear one, over murmurs and guile,
Those who inflict wounds on you are unworthy
of a smile.
It is perfectly acceptable to slumber in the
darkness, embraced by solitude,
For within the realm of dreams, a sanctuary
awaits your mood.

Cast aside the yearning to appease those who make incessant demands,
Your value is not determined by an unforgiving hand.
Be unfettered, be inquisitive, let your essence soar,
The truest reflection of you is precious beyond compare.

Tranquil slumber now, little one, for I am here beside you,
Guiding you with gentle care, with a love that forever stays true.
Dream of fantastical expeditions, where benevolence holds sway, And awaken with the knowledge that you are forever cherished and forever bold.

I've lived…

I've lived in more books, than I've lived
anywhere else,
I've lived more in the friction, between the dusty
journal pages and my pen,

I've lived in more night skies, full of stars
showing me signs,
I've lived more in the backseat of a car,
feverently typing in the notes,

I've lived in more songs, that I add to my playlist
than any other place,
I've lived more in the aroma, of freshly brewed
coffee inside a library,

I've lived in more deliriums, fruiting from my
spectacularly scrutinizing thoughts,
I've lived more in the intermittent swirls, the
blues from the starry nights,

I've lived in more metaphors, from the poems I
write,
I've lived more in the dark of the night, under the
glimmer of the fairy lights, lightly scratching
forlorn tunes,

Lately, I've lived more for that one moment,
where I've lived the most with me...

trepidezza

in the face of shadows, doubt's cold sting,
how dare I dream of a brighter spring?
to weave a hope from threads so frail,
a defiance whispered, a whispered exhale.

how dare I trust, after trust betrayed,
in hearts that faltered, in promises swayed?
to reach for a friend, hand outstretched,
though scars remain, a lesson etched.

kindness killed them…

There once was a benevolent soul,
Whose kindness made the broken heart whole,
Their compassion knew no end,
To everyone they called friend,
Yet in solitude, they bore a heavy toll...

As days turned to months and then years,
Their altruism caused them fear,
For the world seemed to forget,
That kindness to them was a debt,
A truth that brought their eyes to tears...

beyond the Rose-Kissed veil

Through rose-kissed panes, the world
transformed,
A gilded cage where beauty swarmed.
Imperfect hues to brilliance wrought,
Harsh dissonance to symphony caught.

In every flaw, a veiled delight,
A tapestry woven, warm and bright.
Love's tender gaze, unclouded, clear,
Exalted all it held most dear.

But whispers crept, the veil grew thin,
Reality's harsh light seeped within The heart,
once sheltered, felt the blow,
Of shattered dreams, a world askew.

We mourn the solace, the rose's spell,
The haven where all imperfections fell.
Yet, linger still the echoes faint,
Of a beauty born of no constraint.

For in the rose's fading hue,
A deeper wisdom shimmers through.
The power of perception's art
To mend the broken, mend the heart.

inadequately ENOUGH !

On a scale of,
Nothing at all to a little too much,
I somehow feel.
Just inadequately enough...
I guess, I finally,
Understand the moon...
Somedays,
He's far from complete,
All by himself,
Yet, shining his innocence,
Borrowed from the sun, perhaps.
But even with craters and imperfections,
He casts a certain magic,
A soft, hopeful glow.
And maybe, just maybe,
That's enough.
Because even though I might feel
A little chipped around the edges,
A little too much or not quite there,
I can still shine my own light,
Borrowed from the experiences that make me,
me.

a·pet·al·ous

Once, a rose bloomed vibrant, its petals aflame,
Tended by a gardener, whispers spoke their
name.
Love, a gentle rain, nourished both the flower,
And the one who nurtured it, every passing hour.

But the gardener's call grew strong, distant fields
to claim,
Leaving the rose to weather the sun's scorching
flame.
Responsibilities bloomed, a garden overgrown,
The rose, once cherished, felt distant and alone.

Friends, like butterflies, flitted by in carefree
ease,
While the rose, rooted deep, longed for the
whispering breeze.
Conversations dwindled, a language half-forgot,
The love that bloomed freely, seemed to wither
in a pot.

Can love survive alone, when passions turn to
dust?
Can a rose take solace in memories, and trust?

undeRstudy's grace

In gilded replies, you paint a life unmarred,
Yet grace finds its form in the flaws we've bard.
The dais, a dream, yet unseen wings hold might,
For even the understudy learns the star's celestial
flight.

The fissures in the facade, the tumbles and the
falls,
These are the hushed refrains through vacant
vaudeville halls.
So we'll bide in the wings, our spirits no less
keen,
For the essence of the play throbs vibrant,
unseen.

this thing in my chest…

This little drummer in my ribs, a caffeinated maelstrom,
pounds out a cacophony of whims, a symphony of maybes,
The world outside, awash in an ethereal blush,
every vagrant feline an escapade, each puddle a potential proscenium.
It whispers sagas of grand pronouncements, whispered secrets,
tugging at my sleeve, a small kid tugging at my theatrical gown.
Though persistent in its yearnings, a relentless sweetness,
a field of wildflowers swaying in the zephyr's caress.
Delicate, undoubtedly, yet not readily fractured,
a ferocious tenderness that brooks no dismissal.

This thing in my chest, it wants what it wants.

the Void

Cracked mosaic floor of my being,
each tile a face loved too hard,
shattered remnants scattered underfoot,
souvenirs of generosity gone wrong.
I bled sunsets for strangers,
poured galaxies into eyes that wandered,
offered constellations of whispered secrets,
each whispered hope, stolen clean.

The ache, a hollow echo in the canyons of my
chest,
where laughter used to play,
where dreams hung tapestries of impossible
futures,
stolen like prized tapestries,
leaving bare ribs exposed,
wind whistling through broken windows of my
soul.

They call me naive,
a bleeding tapestry in a cynical world,
a heart overflowing in a desert of
self-preservation.
But what else can I be?

To turn myself inside out, a fist of thorns held
close,
is to suffocate the sunrise in my blood,
extinguish the moonbeam in my bones.

So I walk, mosaic heart held high,
a constellation of scars like a warrior's map,
a testament to loving fiercely,
even when it leaves me bare.
This void, it is not an emptiness,
but a canvas carved by storms,
an invitation for the universe to paint its vibrant
chaos within.

I will gather starlight in my palms,
weave moonbeams into tapestries of resilience,
learn to bloom not despite the cracks,
but within them, wild and unyielding.
This mosaic life, it is mine to own,
a broken symphony still humming with defiance,
a testament to a love that cannot be stolen, only
reshaped.

For even in the echo of absence,
my spirit burns, a supernova in the night,
a reminder that sometimes,
the most beautiful art is found in the pieces left
behind.

And I will live, mosaic and all, a kaleidoscope of
scars and stardust, a love story written in broken
fragments, forever aglow.

Epilogue

Dusk drapes her fiery shawl upon the sky,
Where my odyssey's chronicle surrenders to the
sand.
Each grain, a whispered glyph of joy and
sorrow's sigh,
Carved upon the shore, where memory makes its
stand.

The ravenous tide, a fickle god, devours the past,
Its salty tongue erasing tales with each retreating
lick.
The ground I roamed, a canvas ever recast,
No map remains to guide your soul's intrepid
pick.

Yet, where sea meets sky in a shimmering
mirage,
A tapestry of futures dances to the wind's soft
call.
Footsteps yet unwritten, whispered on the page,
Borne on ocean's breath, awaiting one and all.

A child's laughter, a seashell's pearly chime,
A lover's hand, a bond that time itself can't
sever.

A mountain scaled, a brushstroke kissed with
sublime,
These ripples echo, safe from Neptune's hungry
fever.

Though sands of time may shift and stories
wane,
Untrodden paths beckon, where dreams unfurl,
unbound.
So let the waves wash clean, let whispers weave
again,
For in each fading mark, your future's light is
found.

Anabasis

Rayna,
a wisp of a child at barely five years old,
faltered before the imposing edifice.
The grand staircase,
crafted from mahogany burnished to an obsidian
sheen,
ascended in a sinuous coil,
mimicking a slumbering serpent.
Sunlight,
filtered through grime-encrusted panes high
above,
cast motes in the air,
each particle a clandestine whisper.
The inherited house, a labyrinthine sprawl,
boasted a plethora of such staircases,
each a gateway to veiled recesses.

This one, however,
possessed a distinct aura.
It pulsed with a subdued energy,
an irresistible pull that Rayna,
with her nascent inquisitiveness,
couldn't ignore. Inhaling deeply,
she grasped the tarnished brass railing,
its coolness a stark counterpoint to the feverish
anticipation thrumming within her.

The initial step emitted a mournful creak,
a sound promptly devoured by the cavernous
silence of the house.
Upward she ventured,
each hesitant step an act of intrepid exploration.

With each ascended tier,
the ambiance morphed into one of sepulchral
gloom.
Cobwebs,
like diaphanous shrouds,
brushed against her face,
and the air grew thick with the weight of
forgotten years.
Whispers,
seemingly emanating from the shrouded corners,
narrated tales of a lifelong extinguished.
Fear was an alien concept to Rayna;
she was consumed by an insatiable curiosity.
These weren't phantoms lurking beneath the
stairs,
but rather spectral echoes of a life well-lived,
a bygone era yearning to be unearthed.

One landing gave way to another,
each one unveiling a forgotten relic: a porcelain
doll,
marred by chips but imbued with a melancholic
charm;

a faded tapestry depicting a fantastical realm lost
to time;
a dusty trunk overflowing with aged missives
bound by ribbons the color of faded dreams.
Each artifact,
a tangible fragment of a life half-remembered,
a hushed utterance in a forgotten narrative.

Finally,
she reached the apogee.
The attic,
a realm unto itself,
overflowed with caskets brimming with
discarded dreams and endeavors left unfinished.
In the epicenter stood a rocking chair,
swaying rhythmically as if propelled by an
unseen hand.
Rayna settled into its embrace, the worn fabric a
cool caress against her skin.

Gazing down at the serpentine path she'd
traversed,
a profound sense of tranquility washed over her.
The whispers that had initially seemed ominous
now resembled forgotten lullabies.
The labyrinthine complexities of the house
mirrored the intricate convolutions of her own
mind,

the attics of her own consciousness brimming
with unspoken thoughts and concealed
aspirations.

As the sun dipped below the horizon,
casting elongated shadows across the attic floor,
Rayna grasped the nascent recognition that this
exploration was merely the commencement of a
grand odyssey.
The once daunting staircases now beckoned,
each step a descent into the labyrinth of her own
being,
a voyage of self-discovery just beginning.

The little girl who had faltered at the foot of the
stairs had,
with each ascended tier,
transcended into a being of burgeoning wisdom.
The complexities that had initially induced
trepidation now held the key to unraveling the
mysteries of her own self.
The grand staircase wasn't merely a passageway,
but a cartographical inscription,
guiding her not only through the enigmatic halls
of the house,
but also through the uncharted territories of her
own mind.